PAIDEIA EDUCATION

JANE AUSTEN

Sense and Sensibility

Literary analysis

Paideia Education

© Paideia Education.

1 rue Honoré - 93500 Pantin (France)
ISBN 978-2-7593-0702-9
Legal Deposit: august 2020

Printing Books on Demand GmbH

In de Tarpen 42

22848 Norderstedt (Deutschland)

CONTENTS

- Author's biography... 9

- Work presentation..15

- Summary.. 19

- Reasons of success.. 37

- Main themes.. 45

- Analysis of the literary movement............................... 57

AUTHOR'S BIOGRAPHY

On December 16, 1775, Jane Austen was born in Great Britain, in the county of Hampshire. Her father, William George Austen, was a clergyman. Her mother, born Cassandra Leigh, was of aristocratic origin. The Austen family belonged to the minor gentry. Jane had six brothers—James, George, Edward, Henry, Francis, and Charles—and one elder sister, Cassandra.

In 1782, the two sisters were sent to Oxford, where a governess named Ann Cawley took charge of their education. They followed her to Southampton and then to Reading, where a typhus epidemic broke out. The two sisters were quickly sent back home. In 1785, they were sent to boarding school, where they learned French, embroidery, dancing, music, and sewing. In December 1786, their parents could no longer afford their schooling. They returned to the rectory while their brothers continued studying at Oxford.

William George Austen owned a library of five hundred books and gave his daughters unrestricted access to it. He also provided them with writing materials, which were expensive at the time. Fond of reading, the Austen family often read aloud together in the evenings after dinner. They also enjoyed the theater, and the siblings amused themselves by writing and performing plays.

Jane began writing as early as 1787. Her earliest works were later grouped under the title Juvenilia, which notably includes the epistolary novel *Love and Friendship* and the historical piece *The History of England*. These were parodies of sentimental and historical novels.

Jane wrote, read, and devoted herself to other artistic pursuits. As an accomplished young woman, she helped her mother manage the household. In the evenings, she read her own writings aloud to the family. These readings inspired her to pursue a career as a writer. Between 1793 and 1795, she wrote a short epistolary novel, *Lady Susan*.

In 1795, she devoted herself to writing a second novel in the same literary genre, *Elinor and Marianne*. That same year, she met Thomas Langlois Lefroy, a law graduate without fortune. Since Jane had no dowry, the Lefroy family sent the young man away.

In 1796, she wrote her first novel, *First Impressions*, which she completed a year later. Her family greatly appreciated the novel, and her father attempted to have it published, but Thomas Cadell, a publisher of the time, rejected it.

Jane Austen then returned to *Elinor and Marianne*, reshaped it into a full novel, and changed its title to *Sense and Sensibility*.

She next wrote *Susan*, which would later become *Northanger Abbey*, a parody of the Gothic novel, a literary genre very fashionable at the time. Henry, her brother a year older than she, managed to sell *Susan* to the publisher Benjamin Crosby. However, he allowed the novel to fall into oblivion.

In 1800, the Austen family moved to Bath, in the county of Somerset. In 1802, Jane Austen received what appears to have been her only marriage proposal. She initially accepted but later refused.

In 1804, she began a novel titled *The Watsons*, which she abandoned after the death of William George Austen in 1805. During this period, the mother and daughters found themselves in a precarious financial situation. The Austen sons provided financial assistance. In 1806, Francis ("Frank") was able to host his mother and sisters. In 1809, Edward offered them a cottage on his estate called Chawton House.

Cassandra and Jane were considered old maids: Cassandra had lost her fiancé, who died of fever in Saint-Domingue, and Jane apparently never had a serious suitor. They devoted themselves to the duties expected of their social status, caring for the poor and the sick and managing the household. Jane also returned to writing.

In 1809, Jane Austen was able to buy back *Susan* from Benjamin Crosby.

Her novel *Sense and Sensibility* was accepted by Thomas Egerton and published in November 1811.

She then published *First Impressions* under a new title, *Pride and Prejudice*, with the same publisher in June 1813. The work received a warmer reception than the previous one.

In 1812, she began writing *Mansfield Park*, which was published in 1814. However, this novel met with less success than the others.

In 1815, she changed publishers and released her fifth novel, *Emma*. She was reportedly advised to dedicate it to George IV, which she did without much enthusiasm. Nevertheless, the book was very well received, and the Prince Regent appreciated the gesture.

In 1816, Jane began writing *The Elliots*, later titled *Persuasion*. That same year, Henry went bankrupt and fell into debt. He and his brothers could no longer support their mother and sisters financially. Jane's health began to deteriorate rapidly. She nevertheless continued writing, completed *The Elliots*, and then began *The Brothers*, which she did not have time to finish. Jane Austen died on July 18, 1817, at the age of forty-one.

Cassandra and Henry Austen had *Persuasion* and *Northanger Abbey* published together by John Murray in December 1817. Jane Austen's anonymity ended with the "Biographical Notice" written by her brother and included in the volume. Although sales were initially good, they eventually declined. Twelve years later, Richard Bentley republished all of Jane Austen's novels in his "Standard Novels" collection.

WORK PRESENTATION

In 1795, Jane Austen devoted herself to writing *Elinor and Mariann*, a novel whose title she changed a year later to *Sense and Sensibility*. This novel was first written in epistolary form before the author transformed it into a narrative style, which became third-person narration.

It is Jane Austen's first published novel. It was published by Thomas Egerton at the author's expense on October 30, 1811, but anonymously. Jane Austen, out of concern for her reputation, could not present herself as the author. However, the novel received a favorable reception and was even translated in 1815 by Isabelle de Montolieu. The first print run was between 750 and 1000 copies. The second took place in 1813.

The main themes are contained in the title of the novel. They are reason and passion, two different ways of loving. Elinor represents reason and Marianne emotion.

SUMMARY

Chapter 1

Henry Dashwood lives with his uncle, Mr. Dashwood, at the Norland estate, located in Sussex, with his wife and their three daughters, Elinor, Marianne, and Margaret. Henry Dashwood has a son, John, born from a first marriage. The latter is married and enjoys a comfortable life. Upon his uncle's death, Henry Dashwood had hoped that he would leave the greater part of his fortune to the girls, but it ultimately goes to John and his son Harry. Henry Dashwood cannot remedy the situation, and before dying himself, he asks his son to look after the family. John plans to provide financial assistance to the Dashwoods.

Chapter 2

John Dashwood, his wife Fanny, née Ferrars, and their son Harry settle at Norland. Fanny considers herself the mistress of the estate, but the furniture belongs, to her great displeasure, to the Dashwood women. The latter are disparaged by the young woman, who dissuades her husband from giving them too large a sum of money.

Chapter 3

Mrs. Dashwood sees her relationship with Fanny deteriorate and looks for lodging near Norland. She is unaware of the decision made by her late husband regarding the financial assistance owed to her by her stepson. Elinor, for her part, gets along well with Edward, her sister-in-law's younger brother. This delights Mrs. Dashwood, while Marianne finds the young man far too dull.

Chapter 4

Elinor does not know whether her feelings for Edward are love, while her mother and sister already think about this future marriage. Fanny makes Mrs. Dashwood understand that her own family refuses the idea of Edward marrying a girl without fortune. Mrs. Dashwood wishes more than ever to leave Norland with her daughters. She receives a letter from a distant relative, Sir John Middleton, who offers them the opportunity to live in the village of Barton, in Devonshire. Mrs. Dashwood accepts after receiving the agreement of her daughters, and particularly that of Elinor.

Chapter 5

John and his wife learn of the imminent departure of the Dashwood women. Mrs. Dashwood thus wishes to distance her eldest daughter from Edward. She realizes that her stepson will not keep the promise made to Henry Dashwood. She and her daughters leave Norland with great sorrow.

Chapter 6

Barton Cottage is a comfortable dwelling. Practical-minded, Mrs. Dashwood already thinks about the future arrangements of the house. Cordial, Sir John Middleton comes to visit them and invites them to call on him and his wife. Lady Middleton shows coldness and reserve while remaining polite.

Chapter 7

The Middletons enjoy receiving guests, especially Sir John. He shows concern for the comfort of his relatives. The Dashwood women also meet Lady Middleton's mother, Mrs. Jennings, and a friend of the Middletons, Colonel Brandon. Marianne looks indulgently upon the colonel, whom she considers old even though he is not yet forty.

Chapter 8

Mrs. Jennings proves to be a matchmaker. She has noticed the colonel's feelings for Marianne and continually makes remarks about it, despite the young girl's indignation. Marianne seriously believes that the colonel is too old to live a love story.

Chapter 9

The Dashwoods appreciate the Middleton family but wish to maintain their independence. During a walk with Margaret, Marianne twists her ankle. A young stranger carries her back to the house. His name is Willoughby and he lives at Allenham with a cousin, Mrs. Smith. The Dashwoods wish to obtain more information about him from their cousin, but Sir John provides them with little. He prefers to speak of the colonel, whom he would like to see married to Marianne.

Chapter 10

Willoughby visits Marianne daily and seems to appreciate her passionate and exalted character. Elinor certainly likes the young man but is apprehensive about certain aspects of his character. She has also noticed the colonel's attraction to her sister and defends him when Marianne and Willoughby mock him and show contempt toward him.

Chapter 11

Sir John constantly organizes receptions, outings, and country parties. Marianne and Willoughby behave exclusively in their relationship and openly display their interest in each other, to Elinor's great embarrassment. The colonel is hurt by Marianne's indifference.

Chapter 12

Willoughby has offered a horse to Marianne. She is at first delighted before being brought back to reason by her elder sister. Indeed, the animal can only cause financial problems. Marianne tells Elinor that she is engaged to Willoughby, to whom she has given a lock of her hair. An outing is planned for the next day to Whitwell, where Colonel Brandon's brother-in-law resides.

Chapter 13

The colonel must leave suddenly for London. The excursion is therefore canceled. Marianne and Willoughby are mocking, Sir John tries to detain the colonel, and Mrs. Jennings is indiscreet. The colonel leaves without any explanation. Elinor learns that her sister has gone alone with Willoughby to Allenham. She tries to encourage Marianne to show more restraint, in vain.

Chapter 14

Mrs. Jennings remains curious about the colonel's departure. Marianne and Willoughby grow closer and closer, even though the young people are of modest means. Willoughby also shows great attachment to the young girl's family.

Chapter 15

Upon returning from a walk, Mrs. Dashwood, Elinor, and Margaret notice Marianne's sorrow and learn of Willoughby's departure for London. Each offers a hypothesis. Mrs. Dashwood thinks that the young man's relative wishes to separate him from her daughter, who lacks fortune. Elinor believes there has been a quarrel between the young people.

Chapter 16

There seems to be no correspondence between Marianne and Willoughby. The young girl is in the grip of great sorrow and deliberately isolates herself. Convinced of Willoughby's return, she mistakes him for Edward, who comes to visit the Dashwood family. The young man initially appears somewhat distant, especially with Elinor.

Chapter 17

The Dashwood women learn that Edward has no intention of becoming an orator, as his family had planned. He is, however, very wealthy.

Chapter 18

Marianne remains dismayed by Edward's lack of imagination and passion. She remarks aloud that he is wearing a ring containing a lock of hair. She and Margaret think it belongs to Elinor, although the young man seems very embarrassed.

Chapter 19

Edward remains resigned to his idleness and the fact that he neither works nor has any occupation. After his departure, Elinor refuses to give in to grief so as not to worry her mother and sisters. Charlotte Palmer—Lady Middleton's sister—and her husband come to visit their family. The Dashwood sisters are obliged to accept a dinner invitation at the Middletons'.

Chapter 20

Mrs. Palmer insists that the two sisters come and visit her. The Palmers have a house at Cleveland and know Willoughby. They live near him. Curiously, they speak of the forthcoming marriage between Willoughby and Marianne. They praise Willoughby but also Colonel Brandon, who nearly married Charlotte Palmer.

Chapter 21

The Steele sisters, distant cousins of the Jennings family, visit the Middletons. The elder, Anne, is foolish and talkative, while Lucy is calculating and sly. They nevertheless please Lady Middleton by complimenting her children, who are in fact very ill-mannered. They displease the Dashwood sisters, who do not appreciate their hypocrisy. Anne claims to know Edward, to Elinor's great surprise.

Chapter 22

Lucy likes Elinor, but her lack of education, manners, and pride is obvious. She is overly servile and flattering. Lucy tells Elinor that she has been secretly engaged to Edward for four years. She shows her a portrait of the young man. The hair in the ring belongs to Lucy, and the young people constantly write to each other. Elinor is devastated.

Chapter 23

Elinor senses that Lucy is jealous of her, because Edward continually compliments her. The Dashwood sisters are bored during women's gatherings, where frivolity, foolishness, and flattery prevail. During a game of whist, Elinor arranges to speak with Lucy again.

Chapter 24

Lucy comes from a more modest background than her fiancé, which explains her interest in his fortune. Elinor is not deceived and makes this clear to her. Lucy does not hesitate to ask Elinor to intercede with her brother so that Edward may be appointed preacher at the Norland parsonage. Her audacity and greed make her less agreeable in Elinor's eyes, who decides to distance herself.

Chapter 25

Mrs. Jennings insists on taking Marianne and Elinor to stay with her near Portman Square, in London. While Marianne is enthusiastic at the thought of seeing Willoughby again, Elinor dreads encountering Edward. She also fears having to endure Mrs. Jennings's company.

Chapter 26

Marianne shows ingratitude toward Mrs. Jennings, and her sister expresses gratitude on behalf of both of them. A few days after her arrival, Marianne writes a letter to Willoughby and constantly expects him to visit. She is therefore terribly disappointed when she learns of the colonel's arrival.

Chapter 27

Like her son-in-law, Mrs. Jennings constantly receives visitors. Colonel Brandon regularly comes to speak with Elinor and to see Marianne, with whom he is still in love. Marianne's agitation increases when she learns that Willoughby has visited Mrs. Jennings and left his card. The Middletons also come to London and stay in Conduit Street. They organize an evening gathering, and Marianne learns that Willoughby was invited but did not attend. The colonel informs Elinor that Marianne and Willoughby's engagement is known to everyone.

Chapter 28

At an evening gathering at the Middletons', the Dashwood sisters meet Willoughby. He behaves coldly toward Marianne, to her great distress. He remains indifferent, though courteous, and quickly takes his leave. Marianne is desperate, and Elinor is horrified and believes the young man has broken his promise of marriage.

Chapter 29

Elinor realizes that the rumor of her sister's engagement and marriage to Willoughby was spread by Mrs. Jennings. The latter is still unaware of Willoughby's actions. The young man has written a letter to Marianne in which he presents their story as a misunderstanding. He returns her letters and her ring. The young girl is devastated and tells her sister that their relationship was not truly official. She gives herself up to grief.

Chapter 30

Mrs. Jennings understands her mistake when she learns of Willoughby's impending marriage to a certain Miss Grey. For once, she shows discretion toward Marianne and seeks to provide her with distraction. Elinor learns that Miss Grey is very wealthy and tells Mrs. Jennings that she wishes her family to avoid any reference to Willoughby in front of her sister. Colonel Brandon, who has learned the news, shows attentiveness toward Marianne.

Chapter 31

Mrs. Dashwood is unaware of the breakup and writes to Marianne, rejoicing over her relationship with Willoughby. The colonel tells Elinor of his love for a distant cousin, Eliza, who had in fact been destined for his brother. After a painful separation, the young woman fell into ruin. She dies, leaving her daughter Eliza to the colonel, who placed her in boarding school. The colonel then reveals that Eliza, as a teenager, was seduced by Willoughby, who made her lose her honor before abandoning her.

Chapter 32

Marianne learns the story and shows patience toward the colonel while feeling deep disillusionment toward Willoughby. The Middletons, the Palmers, and Mrs. Jennings display an overwhelming compassion regarding Marianne's story. She learns of Willoughby's marriage from Elinor. Willoughby then leaves London with his young wife. The Steele sisters have managed to settle at Mrs. Jennings's house, and Anne insists too much on seeing Marianne. She is put in her place by Lucy, while Elinor strives to remain patient.

Chapter 33

The Dashwood sisters go shopping and meet their brother John. He is very eager to meet their acquaintances, whom he knows to be wealthy. He also wishes to see his sister Elinor married to the colonel, whom he knows to be rich. Elinor learns that Edward's family intends to have him marry a Miss Morton. John is mean, foolish, stubborn, and ridiculous.

Chapter 34

John and Fanny Dashwood invite the Dashwood sisters and their acquaintances. The Steele sisters are also present, but Elinor does not mention Edward's family's marriage plans. Mrs. Ferrars is present and behaves odiously toward Elinor, much to the latter's amusement. Marianne, however, highly sensitive, vigorously defends her sister. The Dashwoods do not show the eagerness of the Steele sisters, to their brother's great indignation.

Chapter 35

As the Ferrars women greatly appreciate her, Lucy is convinced that the future announcement of her relationship with Edward will not cause any problems. Blinded by her self-satisfaction and success, she does not listen to Elinor. Edward appears. Marianne is warm toward him, convinced that he still wishes to marry her sister. Lucy is deeply displeased. Edward leaves quickly, followed by Lucy. Elinor cannot confide their story to Marianne, as she has promised Lucy to say nothing.

Chapter 36

Charlotte Palmer gives birth to a baby boy. Mrs. Jennings therefore entrusts the Dashwood sisters to Lady Middleton in order to help her daughter. They also associate with the Steele sisters without much pleasure, which is mutual. During an evening gathering, Elinor meets Robert Ferrars, Edward's younger brother, a foolish and self-important character. Lucy boasts of being invited to stay with Anne at John and Fanny's house. Elinor thinks that the young woman will succeed in marrying Edward.

Chapter 37

Mrs. Jennings informs Elinor that the relationship between Lucy and Edward has been revealed to Fanny by Anne. Fanny had a nervous breakdown and expelled the Steele sisters from her house, to Mrs. Jennings's great indignation. Marianne learns the news and admires Elinor's courage regarding the love story between the man she loves and Lucy. John Dashwood reveals to his sisters that Mrs. Ferrars has disinherited and banished Edward in favor of Robert before launching into lamentations. Once John has left, Mrs. Jennings and the Dashwood sisters sharply criticize the Ferrars family.

Chapter 38

Lucy is too self-centered and calculating to deserve Edward's sacrifice. During a walk, Elinor is approached by Anne, who tells her that she overheard Edward and Lucy's declarations of love. Elinor is indignant at such indiscretion. She also learns that the Steele sisters are frequenting the Richardsons, wealthy people. Lucy writes a letter to the Dashwood sisters in which she proclaims her love for Edward. Their marriage therefore seems about to take place.

Chapter 39

The Palmers insist that the Dashwood sisters accompany them to Cleveland. Marianne fears encountering Willoughby, but the sisters accept, intending afterward to return fairly quickly to Barton. Colonel Brandon, indignant at Mrs. Ferrars's behavior toward her eldest son, speaks of offering the young man a position as preacher at Delaford, where he resides. He asks Elinor to convey the offer to him.

Chapter 40

Mrs. Jennings has noticed the closeness between Elinor and the colonel and imagines a future marriage between them. Elinor is happy to inform Edward of the position offered by the colonel.

Chapter 41

Lucy, impatient to live with Edward at the Delaford parsonage, already plans to benefit from the colonel's wealth. While Marianne and Mrs. Jennings, for once in agreement, refuse to visit Fanny, who is said to be ill, Elinor goes out of pure politeness. Her brother is astonished to learn of the colonel's action. Fanny has lost her former pride. Robert openly mocks his elder brother.

Chapter 42

John Dashwood still hopes for a future marriage between Elinor and the colonel. The Middleton, Jennings, Palmer, and Dashwood women go alone to Cleveland, where Mr. Palmer and the colonel are to join them a few days later. During a walk, Marianne falls ill.

Chapter 43

Mrs. Jennings and the colonel are the only ones to take Marianne's illness seriously. The Palmers are lodged with neighbors, as Charlotte wishes to protect her child from Marianne's illness. The young girl seems to recover before falling into delirium and calling for her mother, whom the colonel offers to fetch. Mrs. Jennings, anxious and convinced of Marianne's impending death, increases Elinor's distress. Marianne recovers and feels much better. Believing her mother has arrived, Elinor instead finds herself face to face with Willoughby, who has let himself in.

Chapter 44

Willoughby is relieved to learn that Marianne is feeling better. He admits that he was charmed by Marianne but that the attraction of money prevailed, hence his marriage to Miss Sophia Grey. He attempts to shift responsibility regarding the situation of Eliza, the colonel's ward. Elinor learns that the letter of rejection was written by Miss Grey. Moved by compassion, the young woman confronts him with his responsibilities, and Willoughby appears resigned.

Chapter 45

Elinor hastens to reassure her mother about Marianne's condition. Mrs. Dashwood has spoken extensively with Colonel Brandon and knows of his feelings for her younger daughter. She appreciates the colonel's character more than that of Willoughby.

Chapter 46

Marianne expresses her gratitude to the colonel. The Dashwoods return to Barton. Marianne refuses to weep any longer over her breakup with Willoughby. She also realizes her selfishness and promises her sister to improve herself. Elinor finally tells her about Willoughby's visit and his words.

Chapter 47

Mrs. Dashwood in turn learns of it and judges the young man too frivolous, calculating, and selfish. Mrs. Dashwood and Marianne recognize their former thoughtlessness. The Dashwoods learn of Lucy's marriage from a servant. Marianne suffers for her sister, who strives to control herself. Mrs. Dashwood acknowledges her eldest daughter's courage.

Chapter 48

Edward's unexpected arrival at Barton surprises the Dashwoods. He informs them of Lucy's marriage to Robert, to Elinor's great happiness. The young people are happy.

Chapter 49

Edward had long ceased loving Lucy, and his engagement had been due to his naivety. Mrs. Ferrars has not succeeded in removing Lucy from her family, but she insists that the young woman will never be acknowledged as her daughter-in-law. The financial issue arises for Elinor and Edward, even though he hopes to obtain money from his mother. He resists the idea of submitting, but Elinor's advice makes him reflect.

Chapter 50

Mrs. Ferrars again tries to persuade her eldest son to marry Miss Morton but must resign herself. She has distanced herself from Lucy, who is too servile and too calculating to her taste. Robert wished to mock his brother; Lucy was more interested in money than in feelings, and the couple constantly quarrel. Elinor marries Edward, and the couple lives happily at the Delaford parsonage. Marianne agrees to marry Colonel Brandon. Willoughby forms an idealized image of Marianne after learning of her marriage.

REASONS
OF SUCCESS

Jane Austen lived during the Georgian era, a period so called under the successive reigns of Kings George I, George II, George III and George IV between 1714 and 1830. Certain social changes, not recounted by the author, took place, such as the abolition of slavery, the creation of hospitals and orphanages, and prison reform. It was also a period of war. For several centuries, Europe had colonized the African, American, Australian, and Asian continents. Great Britain was the leading colonial power, notably with colonies in North America and India. But the American colonists eventually rebelled and launched the War of Independence, with the British on one side and the insurgents supported by France on the other. In 1783, Great Britain lost its thirteen colonies. In 1803, Napoleonic France declared war on Great Britain. A defeat for Napoleon I followed in November 1815. Great Britain, which had retained its colonies in India and Ireland, regained its place as a great colonial empire and dominated Europe until 1914, on the eve of the First World War.

In literature, Jane Austen turned to the novel, a genre particularly appreciated during the eighteenth century and throughout the nineteenth century, first in Great Britain, then in Germany and France. It did not have the noble status of poetry but was highly sought after by the educated minority of the population. It was especially read by women. Female authors even devoted themselves to novel writing, such as Ann Radcliffe, Charlotte Lennox, Fanny Burney, and Jane Austen. However, writing a novel as a woman brought certain disadvantages. Women first had to preserve their reputation in society. Moreover, their male counterparts did not appreciate the arrival of women in the literary world. Finally, writing a novel under one's own name as a woman did not give the most serious impression. This is why some women published anonymously, like Jane Austen, and others adopted male pseudonyms, such as Mary Ann Evans, who became George Eliot.

Jane Austen lived at a time when Romanticism predominated; it was the movement par excellence from the end of the eighteenth century until the first half of the nineteenth century. Romanticism was the continuation of pre-Romanticism, where one already notices the beginning of a desire to oppose Classicism. The Gothic novel is a narrative genre that emerged with pre-Romanticism and continued under Romanticism. Horace Walpole was the first author of Gothic novels with *The Castle of Otranto*. It aroused enthusiasm until the 1830s.

Unlike Classicism, where man controls his passions, pre-Romanticism and the Gothic novel bring out the most extreme negative feelings. Horror, terror, downfall, and passion predominate. Many women were passionate about this genre, both in reading and writing. For example, Ann Radcliffe with *The Mysteries of Udolpho*, Charlotte Smith with *Emmeline* and *Celestina*, Eleanor Sleath with *The Orphans of the Rhine*, etc. Men also wrote in this genre: William Thomas Beckford with *Vathek*, Matthew Gregory Lewis with *The Monk*.

Then Romanticism appeared first in Germany in the 1770s, then in Great Britain, where it gradually declined in the 1830s. In the nineteenth century, it spread to France, Italy, and Spain. The poet and novelist wished to express melancholy, torment, sadness, and the "I" prevailed. Passion and sensitivity were expressed, and there was an interest in exoticism. British Romanticism turned back to the Middle Ages as well as to Celtic legends. Novels appeared such as *Rob Roy*, *Ivanhoe*, and *Waverley* by Walter Scott, and *Tom Jones* by Henry Fielding. Even after the decline of Romanticism and the Gothic novel, authors such as the Brontë sisters, Charlotte and Emily, were still influenced by it in their writings *Jane*

Eyre and *Wuthering Heights*.

Until her death, Jane Austen published her novels anonymously. Her identity was revealed after her death by her brother Henry Austen. Although the public welcomed her novels favorably, her contemporaries were less interested. Walter Scott and Richard Whately were among the few authors to recognize her talent during her lifetime. Elizabeth Barrett Browning judged her writing more severely: "She reaches perfection in what she undertakes... but her excellence, it seems to me, lies more in execution than in aspiration. Her view of life is narrow, earthly, and essentially unpoetical." For the adherents of Romanticism, Jane Austen's novels did not correspond to literary ideals. The characters control their feelings and rely on reason; they live in a small society they frequent prudently. The young woman seemed far too artificial in her writing and expressed no passion. Charlotte Brontë was just as unenthusiastic as her fellow writer toward Jane Austen's novel.

Her descriptive and realistic writing brings Jane Austen closer to the literary movement of Realism, whose forerunners in the eighteenth century were Henry Fielding and Tobias Smollett. This movement would truly develop only in the 1850s. But in those years, critics remained doubtful about Jane Austen: her novels were considered only from a moral perspective. A few authors of the second half of the nineteenth century, however, took an interest in Jane Austen, notably George Eliot and her lover and later husband George Henry Lewes. The movement was still in its early stages: George Eliot seems to have contributed to its establishment in her novels such as *Adam Bede*.

Jane Austen's works aroused real enthusiasm from 1869 onward, when her nephew James Edward Austen-Leigh published *A Memoir of Jane Austen*. Some novelists at the end of the nineteenth century, such as Henry James, admired the style Jane Austen adopted in her descriptions and narrative points of view. A major figure of Realism, Henry James was the author of *The Portrait of a Lady*, *The Tragic Muse*, and *A London Life*. In a letter addressed to his friend George Pellow, the writer praised her style: "Personally, I would have spoken more of her genius – of the extraordinary vividness with which she saw what she saw and of her unconscious acuteness in giving it form. […] In a way, of course, infinitely less explicit, Emma Woodhouse and Anne Elliot give us as great an impression of passion – that celebrated quality – as the heroines of Sand and Balzac."

Virginia Woolf is considered the first great female novelist of the twentieth century and is among the authors who introduced Modernism into literature. In *The Art of Fiction*, she describes the evolution of the novel in Great Britain and expresses her admiration for Jane Austen's talent: "Thus to go from one great writer to another, from Jane Austen to Hardy, from Peacock to Trollope, from Scott to Meredith, is to be wrenched and uprooted, tossed here and there. To read a novel is a difficult and complex art. You must be capable not only of great subtlety of perception but also of great boldness of imagination if you are to make the most of what the novelist – the great artist – gives you."

In her youth, Jane Austen was free in her reading. By educating herself, she learned to criticize and observe. She possessed a great literary culture and knew the authors of previous centuries. She drew inspiration from *The Characters* by Jean de La Bruyère to create comic portraits of characters. *In Northanger Abbey*, Jane Austen parodies the Gothic novel, thus imitating the style of Henry Fielding. She advocates reason over passion and imagination. This idea is also present in *Pride and Prejudice*, where the character of Lydia is devalued. The young girl eloped with a suitor without considering the consequences for her family and herself. Jane also drew inspiration from the style of her female contemporaries, including Fanny Burney, from whom she borrowed free indirect discourse and certain feminist ideas. She appreciated the humor in *The Female Quixote or The Adventures of Arabella*, a novel by Charlotte Lennox. As for sentimentalism, Jane Austen took Samuel Johnson, author of sentimental novels, as a model – though with a certain moderation. The characters show restraint even when confessing their feelings, such as Elizabeth and Darcy. By contrast, the character of Marianne in *Sense and Sensibility* readily indulges in passion and emotional outbursts, to the point of forgetting restraint. Jane Austen was also influenced by Walter Scott, Robert Burns, Maria Edgeworth, etc. She thus drew inspiration from several literary movements and several generations.

MAIN THEMES

The main themes are eponymous with Jane Austen's novel, *Sense and Sensibility*. Reason is embodied by the character of Elinor Dashwood. By contrast, Marianne Dashwood represents passion and emotion. Each of the sisters experiences a love story. Marianne falls in love with Willoughby, who ultimately makes a marriage of convenience. After a dark period, the young woman marries Colonel Brandon, a man older than she is but who loves her with a true love. Elinor meets Edward Ferrars, and the young people seem to share the same feelings. But Elinor learns that he has been engaged for four years to Lucy Steele, something his own family is unaware of. After various adventures, Elinor and Edward are finally able to marry. In the early chapters, the author mainly devotes the narrative to Marianne and her relationship with Willoughby, up to the letter of rupture sent by Sophia Grey, the young man's fiancée. But through this story, which ends badly, another story appears: Elinor's.

Elinor Dashwood is a person endowed with wisdom, and her advice seems valuable. Her mother always turns to her when it comes to making a serious decision: "Elinor, her eldest daughter, whose opinion carried so much weight, possessed a strength of understanding and a clarity of judgment which made her, though only nineteen, her mother's usual counsellor and enabled her to temper very happily the liveliness of Mrs. Dashwood […] her temper was affectionate, and her feelings were strong, but she knew how to govern them. This was a knowledge her mother had yet to learn, and which one of her sisters had resolved never to acquire." There is an allusion here to her younger sister, Marianne, whom we will speak about later. Elinor is therefore a young woman who prefers to listen to reason and knows how to remain mistress of her relationships. Yet trials are imposed on her: her father's death, her lack of fortune, leaving the family home of Norland, Edward Ferrars's departure from Barton, and his supposed marriage to Lucy Steele. This nevertheless makes her determined always to control herself and master her emotions. When she learns, from Lucy herself, of the relationship Lucy has with the young man, despite the feeling of despair, she manages to control herself so that Lucy suspects nothing: "For a few moments, she was almost overcome, her heart sinking, and she could hardly stand; but it was absolutely necessary to command herself, and she reacted so vigorously against her feeling of oppression that her success was quick and, for the moment, complete." (Chapter 22). She later learns, from a servant, of Lucy's marriage to a Mr. Ferrars: "Elinor, who, though still much disturbed, had recovered enough composure and voice to ask Thomas about the source of his information." (Chapter 48). The young woman, despite the painful trial still imposed on her, chooses to face reality and to master herself to the end, at least in public. And when Edward arrives, at a moment when she believes he has come to announce his marriage, she wants to control herself to the end: "I must be calm. I will remain mistress of myself." (Chapter 48).

When Edward leaves Barton, she prefers to suffer in silence, without informing her mother or her sisters: "But, as she was determined to get the better of it, and not to show that she suffered from Edward's departure more than the rest of the family […] Without hiding from her family, without systematically shutting herself away in solitude to avoid everyone or staying awake all night to give herself up to reflection […]" (Chapter 19). Elinor is thus anxious to avoid upsetting her mother and sister, people who are too sensitive. She therefore takes on the task of not speaking of the misfortunes that happen to her, of keeping them to herself alone. Elinor thus knows that she can rely only on herself: "She was stronger alone, and her good sense supported her so well that her self-command was as certain, her appearance of cheerfulness as invariable as it was possible to imagine under the influence of regrets so poignant and so recent." (Chapter 23). She thus shows courage but also generosity toward her family. She wishes to spare them trials and always takes it upon herself to anticipate events in order to shorten their suffering: "She never relaxed her vigilance to prevent even the name of Willoughby from being mentioned in Marianne's presence. [...] Elinor had the painful duty of announcing his marriage to her sister. She had arranged to be informed as soon as the ceremony had taken place, wishing not to see Marianne learn it from the newspapers she saw her devour every morning." (Chapter 31). She also wants to inform her mother of Marianne's recovery so that she will no longer worry: "Eager to spare her mother even one instant of horrible uncertainty, she ran at once across the hall and reached the front door just in time to receive her in her arms as she entered." (Chapter 45).

Through her courtesy and patience, Elinor helps her sister Marianne to keep up appearances in society. She plays the part required by an idle, frivolous, sometimes self-interested society, while her sister is wholehearted but not conciliatory at all. "To correct the effect of this behavior, Elinor immediately took up the agreeable role she had assigned herself, devoted herself with the greatest attention to Mrs. Jennings, talked with her, laughed with her, and listened to her as much as she could [...]" (Chapter 26).

Her way of telling things reflects her character. She does not seek to pity herself. The point is to move on as quickly as possible without prolonging the pain: "It was a painful task. [...] But, however thankless it was, it had to be done, and Elinor lost no time in undertaking it. [...] Her account was clear and simple, and though it could not be free from emotion, it contained neither violent agitation nor impetuous complaint. She left that to her listener, for Marianne listened with horror […]" (Chapter 37).

When she learns that her sister Marianne is out of danger after a long illness, she can finally give herself over to joy. Her feelings remain inward, however: "Marianne restored to life, to health, to her friends, to her mother—this was an idea that filled her heart with an exquisite happiness and fervent gratitude, but which did not pour itself out in exclamations of joy, in words or laughter. Her satisfaction was wholly internal, strong and silent." (Chapter 43). Her courage is recognized by her mother, Mrs. Dashwood: "She now feared that her poor judgment had made her unjust, indifferent, yes, almost cruel to Elinor; […] forgetting that she had in Elinor a daughter as severely afflicted, and certainly with less responsibility on her part, and with more courage." (Chapter 47). Her mother and sister even recognize the lightness of their past behavior that led them—Marianne in particular—to be careless about the reputation a woman must have. The young woman's reason is acknowledged and valued.

Her happiness is complete when Edward goes to Barton and informs the Dashwood family that Lucy is married not to him, but to his younger brother, Robert Ferrars. Elinor can rejoice, but once again this expression of happiness is silent, once she is alone: "Elinor could bear it no longer. She almost sprang out of the room, and as soon as the door was shut, burst into tears of joy, which seemed as though they would never end." (Chapter 48). Elinor is the intermediary of the narrator and the embodiment of reason, which leads her always to remain mistress of herself. The young woman has had the wisdom to be reasonable and discreet.

Marianne is Elinor's younger sister. From the beginning, she is defined as having a wholehearted, passionate, excessive temperament: "Marianne possessed, in many respects, the same abilities as her sister. She was sensible and clever, but passionate in everything, incapable of moderating either her sorrows or her joys. She was generous, amiable, interesting—everything except prudent." (Chapter 2). Marianne is also very demanding in her choices of people, beginning with the man she will marry. She herself is aware that she asks a great deal: "It would be impossible for me to be happy with a man whose tastes did not in every point coincide with my own. [...] But as for me, if I had been in love with him, it would have broken my heart to hear him read with so little feeling. Mama, the more I see of the world, the more I am convinced that I shall never find a man I can really love. I require so much!" (Chapter 3). With a frank, spontaneous nature, she is very natural. She thus criticizes the behavior imposed by society and expected of women: "Marianne really did not know what to say. She did not wish at any cost to wound her sister's feelings, and yet it was impossible for her to speak against her own thoughts." (Chapter 4); "—Elinor! cried Marianne. [...] I have been too much at my ease, too happy, too frank! I have neglected the usual forms of propriety. I have been open and sincere where I should have been reserved, lacking wit, heavy and disappointing." (Chapter 10); "Marianne remained silent; it was impossible for her to say the contrary of what she thought, even on the most trivial occasions; and consequently it fell to Elinor to lie when politeness required it." (Chapter 21). She thus disregards propriety and prefers natural behavior, in a society where unfortunately a woman must respect certain social codes. Her elder sister therefore takes on the task of managing their social relations. Marianne is wholehearted and refuses to be conciliatory. She sees things in black and white. "Marianne, who had never had much indulgence for anything that bore the color of impertinence and vulgarity, was at that moment particularly ill-disposed to find pleasure in the Steele young ladies or to encourage their advances." (Chapter 22).

Mrs. Dashwood raised her daughters with the idea of marrying for love. Marianne therefore champions this kind of marriage and despises marriages of convenience and interest: "If he married such a woman, there would be nothing shocking in it. It would be a marriage of convenience, and the world would be satisfied. In my eyes it would not be a marriage at all; it would be nothing. It appears to me only as a commercial exchange, in which each seeks his advantage at the other's expense." (Chapter 8). She is unaware, however, of Willoughby's interest in money. The breakup will therefore be very painful. By contrast, she remains indifferent to the colonel's feelings, though he truly loves her: "Colonel Brandon is certainly younger than Mrs. Jennings, but he might still be my father; and if he has never been capable of feelings lively enough to fall in love, it is certainly a long time since he has been capable of feeling them. It is too ridiculous!" (Chapter 8). A young woman with a wholehearted temperament, she gives herself entirely to love, to the point of deliberately forgetting conventions: "Their mutual attachment was not surprising to Elinor. She would only have wished it less openly displayed, and once or twice she ventured to suggest to Marianne the propriety of a little restraint. But Marianne abhorred all concealment when it was not absolutely indispensable; and to suppress the expression of feelings which were in themselves innocent seemed to her a very unnecessary punishment." (Chapter 11). Entirely absorbed in her passion, she does not see that she may lose her reputation, knowing that a woman's reputation is more fragile than a man's: "As Elinor and Marianne walked together the next morning, the latter communicated to her sister a piece of news which, despite all

Elinor already knew of her sister's imprudence and want of judgment, surprised her by its extravagance." (Chapter 12). She becomes so involved in her story with Willoughby that she lacks distance and does not think about the consequences her behavior may bring.

Marianne is a cultivated person, but nonetheless very narrow-minded. She expects everyone to agree with her. She embodies an arrogant youth who almost thinks the world is at her feet: "Marianne, with great abilities and excellent dispositions, was neither rational nor tolerant. She expected others to have the same opinions and the same feelings as herself and judged their actions by the immediate effect produced on her." (Chapter 31). Her elder sister judges Marianne by her behavior and her ideal: "—No," replied Elinor, "her opinions are entirely romantic. […] All her theories have an unfortunate tendency to disregard propriety. And a better knowledge of the world is certainly what I wish for her most!" (Chapter 11). One can see here an allusion by the author to the Romantic movement. Marianne embodies the romantic character par excellence. She is easily prey to strong emotion, sentimentalism, and effusion. We learn that she loves reading novels, a genre little esteemed in the nineteenth century. But reading novels seems to have made her lose awareness of reality: "Marianne, for her part, had had less leisure to contemplate him [Willoughby] […] She had, however, seen enough to join fully in the others' praise, adding the passion she always put into her eulogies. His person and his manner corresponded exactly to what her imagination had always dreamed for a novel hero" (Chapter 9). She has preconceived ideas about love and the sufferings this feeling can bring. This leads her to adopt an almost theatrical behavior: "But, in whatever manner they had parted, her sister's affliction was undeniable, and she [Elinor] felt the tenderest compassion for that violent sorrow to which Marianne did not merely give way to relieve her nerves, but in which she certainly took pleasure and which she believed herself obliged to cultivate. […] Marianne would not have forgiven herself if she could have slept at all the first night after Willoughby's departure. She would have been ashamed to look her family in the face." (Chapter 15).

The breakup with Willoughby plunges the young woman into great despair. After the young man's letter, she gives herself up to "the excess of her affliction," "the excess of her despair"; she has "frequent bursts of grief" and is "almost overcome with sorrow." "That word, as any other would have done, was too much for Marianne, who could only exclaim, in the anguish of her heart, and before bursting into tears:— Oh! Elinor, I am very unhappy!" (Chapter 29). In losing the man she believes she loves, the young woman also loses her romantic illusions: "The violence of her passion had calmed, but she remained sunk in a gloomy dejection. She suffered more from the loss of her illusions about Willoughby's character than she had suffered from the loss of her love." (Chapter 32). Her illness has also led her to draw inspiration from her sister's behavior: "My illness has made me think. It has given me the leisure and calm for a serious examination of conscience. […] I have seen in my conduct, from the beginning of our acquaintance with him last autumn, only a series of imprudences toward myself and a want of consideration for others. I have seen that I was myself the cause of my misfortunes and that my lack of courage in bearing them almost brought me to the grave." (Chapter 46). She therefore returns to reason, which takes hold over emotion.

The young woman—selfish, willful, stubborn—has become more reasonable and attentive, even if her emotions still overwhelm her. When the Dashwood family believes it is Edward who has married Lucy and not Robert, Marianne faints in place of her sister, who manages to control herself. The painful ordeal of the breakup has made her wiser. Her marriage to Colonel Brandon at the end of the novel shows that she has matured and softened.

Sense and Sensibility allows Jane Austen to highlight the feeling of reason. Romanticism is criticized by the author, along with sentimentalism, transports, and effusions in which Marianne willingly indulges. According to Jane Austen, one must not be guided by emotional impulses but listen to reason and control oneself, master oneself. The author does not, however, aim to be Manichean and does not condemn Marianne, who in turn experiences true love.

ANALYSIS OF THE LITERARY MOVEMENT

Under Queen Victoria's reign, major social, economic, and technological changes took place, such as the Industrial Revolution. British Realism therefore had reason to exist during this period. It is the successor to Romanticism, in which the "I," passion, nostalgia, and exoticism were emphasized. By contrast, realist authors turn toward society, its changes, and its events. They present themselves as objective, describing and observing what happens around them as realistically as possible. Description is paramount in comparison with plot and, above all, with the characters' feelings.

In the Victorian era, echoing a conservative and therefore idealistic society, the novel stages characters concerned with propriety within a polished and morally upright society. Female characters in particular are fragile, innocent, and must be protected by a hero. At the same time, some writers are more concerned with describing a society they consider hypocritical, especially regarding women. They criticize the idea of the "marriage market": these are marriages of interest and convenience, not of love. Realist authors are keen to denounce, in particular, social abuses committed against women. A feminist movement is increasingly present in people's minds. In many writers, whether men or women, female characters become more and more vivid. These female figures have a presence: they are sometimes the heroines of the narrative, and their independence makes them more important. They no longer depend on a man. Realism describes marital and family relationships, social problems, and professions. Authors are especially interested in the bourgeois, middle, and working classes.

Realist writers come from different social backgrounds, but all had the opportunity to read and educate themselves. Their way of life scandalizes society at the time: they are single, homosexual, bisexual. They rarely display themselves, preferring discretion. Women are more liberated but remain reserved. In keeping with their writings, which reflect reality and current events, these writers lead lives that detach themselves from the conventional yet abstract ideals of marriage.